A DOCUMENTARY HISTORY OF THE HOLOCAUST™

KRISTALLNACHT AND LIVING IN NAZI GERMANY

ANN BYERS

ROSEN PUBLISHING®
New York

Published in 2015 by The Rosen Publishing Group, Inc.
29 East 21st Street, New York, NY 10010

First Edition

Library of Congress Cataloging-in-Publication Data

Byers, Ann.
Kristallnacht and living in Nazi Germany/Ann Byers. — First edition.
pages cm. — (A documentary history of the Holocaust)
Includes bibliographical references and index.
Audience: Grades 7-12.
ISBN 978-1-4777-7595-0 (library bound)
1. Kristallnacht, 1938—Juvenile literature. 2. Jews—Persecutions—Germany—History—20th century—Juvenile literature. 3. Jews—Germany—History—1933-1945—Juvenile literature. 4. Holocaust, Jewish (1939-1945—Germany—Juvenile literature. 5. Germany—Social conditions—1933-1945—Juvenile literature. I. Title.
DS134.255.B94 2015
940.53'180943—dc23

2013051159

Manufactured in the United States of America

CONTENTS

INTRODUCTION

The Dinslaken Jewish orphanage, established in 1885, served as a social center for the Jews in the small town. These children are studying in one of the orphanage's classrooms during the 1930s.

It was only 6:00 AM, but the bell at the gate of the orphanage was ringing insistently. Cautiously, Yitzhak Herz opened the door. In stomped two Gestapo officers and a policeman in plain clothes. They said they needed to search the orphanage for weapons. As they tore through drawers and lockers, one of the men whispered to Herz, "During the night, all the Jewish men in Dinslaken were arrested."

Fewer than two hundred Jews lived in the small German town. The Jewish orphanage there was more than a home for Jewish orphans. It was also a school for Jewish children from other towns. Their parents hoped they would be safer there than in larger cities where discrimination often erupted in open hostility. On this morning, November 10, 1938, it was no longer a refuge from the violence.

After the police left, Herz, one of the teachers at the orphanage, gathered all thirty-two children and fourteen staff together. At 9:30 the Gestapo came again, this time about fifty of them. They splintered the windows and broke down the doors, ripping huge gashes in the walls. Everything they could lift, they tossed through the openings—books, chairs, tables, a piano. Ignoring the commands of the Nazis, Herz led the sobbing children out a back door and away from the mayhem.

Spotting a group of policemen, he urged his frightened charges toward them. But the officers sneered that they did not protect Jews. Instead, one used his bayonet to herd the group back to the orphanage. He ordered them to stay in the garden behind the building. From there they watched the destruction of their home and school.

They were not the only ones watching; a crowd of several hundred had formed. Herz recognized people he knew: merchants and shopkeepers, people with whom he did business. They were his neighbors. Now they simply stood on the sidewalks, staring in silence.

One of the policemen commanded the children to pile into a hay wagon. Four of the older boys were instructed to pull the cart. Two policemen and brown-shirted Nazis led the "Jew Parade" as it wound through Dinslaken to the jeers of the townspeople who lined the route. Herz could tell that a few in the crowd did not approve, but they stood with the rest, doing nothing.

The parade ended in a small schoolyard near what had been the town's synagogue; now it was a smoldering ruin. All the other Jews in the town were brought to the schoolyard along with the children. They were mostly women who told how their husbands, fathers, and sons had been slapped, kicked, beaten, and taken from them the night before.

This event was one of thousands of horrors inflicted upon Jews throughout Germany and Austria in a single night and day that came to be known as Kristallnacht. Literally "Crystal Night," the name means "Night of Broken Glass." It was not the first instance of violence against Jews in Germany. Neither would it be the last brutality these Jews would endure. It was the beginning of a campaign of terror and savagery unequaled in modern history.

CHAPTER 1

THE FIRE PIT: ANTI-SEMITISM

The coals that burst into flame in Germany in November 1938 had been glowing hot for a long time. Ever since large numbers of Jews came to Europe in the Middle Ages, they encountered people who did not like them. Their cultural practices and religious beliefs were different from those of other Europeans, and people sometimes fear or reject those who are different.

Dislike of Jews was strong in the 1870s, when social Darwinism became popular. Some people applied Darwin's ideas about evolution to people. They sorted humans into different races and stated that some were "fitter," or better than others. This philosophy led to the notion that "Jewish" was not a religious or cultural trait, but a racial designation. Some sociologists decided that the most advanced people were those of the Aryan race. Social Darwinism classified the tall, blonde, blue-eyed Aryan, also called Germanic, Teutonic, or Nordic, as the "master race," and extremists thought of Jews as so inferior that they were not worthy of life.

Any group of people seen as different from the majority can become easy to blame—or used as a

This 1920 Nazi poster is meant to picture a perfect Aryan, representative of Germany, in danger from a hideous man, who represents any and all Jews.

scapegoat, for whatever problems the majority might experience. In the 1920s and 1930s, Germany had a number of problems, and by 1938, many in the country laid the blame for all of them on the Jews.

"BACKSTABBERS"

The first widespread instance of scapegoating came in 1918, toward the end of the Great War, which later became known as World War I. The four-year conflict was a bloody disaster for Germany. It had cost nearly $38 billion and the lives of almost 2.5 million of its citizens. Many Germans had difficulty believing that their mighty army could be defeated. The military commanders refused to admit that they had been beaten in battle; instead, they claimed they had been betrayed by enemies at home. Civilian traitors, they insisted, had sabotaged the war effort. They had disrupted communications, choked off supply lines, and blown up factories that produced armaments. The brave German soldiers had been forced to stop short of victory because the traitors had signed a truce, stabbing them in the back.

Who were the enemies at home? The leaders pointed to left-wing fanatics, primarily Bolsheviks, or Communists, who wanted to overthrow the military government. But they also accused the Jews. Despite the fact that twelve thousand Jews had died defending the Fatherland, newspaper articles, speeches, and political cartoons denounced Jews as the cause of the nation's unexpected loss. Anti-Semites claimed that the nearly one hundred thousand Jews who had fought for Germany did so only for their own profit and intentionally demoralized the soldiers with whom they served.

"CONSPIRATORS"

The stabbed-in-the-back accusation grew quickly into a conspiracy theory that fed the popular notions that Jews were inferior and bent on destroying the more cultured Germans. According to the theory, the Jews in Germany were part of a global network of Jews that controlled the world's financial institutions and wanted to dominate the political structures as well. They started the war to weaken all the European nations so that they could eventually rule them. Toward that end, they were in league with the Bolsheviks, instigating unrest and revolution all across the continent.

The theory inaccurately held that Jews were responsible for the collapse of the German government, the signing of a truce when victory was in sight, and the humiliating terms of the treaty that ended the war. The Treaty of Versailles stripped Germany of large chunks of territory and slashed its military to almost nothing. It demanded that Germany pay reparations—reimburse the winning nations for their costs in waging the war—to the tune of $33 million. Worst of all, it forced the proud nation to admit that Germany and Germany alone was guilty of causing all the devastation of the war. To ease their shame and suffering, German leaders blamed their misery on Jewish conspirators. Although the

After World War I, Germans needed lots of paper money to buy even small things. In a bank in Berlin, this employee is counting bundles of reichsmarks, the German currency.

stabbed-in-the-back conspiracy theory was obviously false, many Germans accepted it as fact.

Conditions in the country worsened in the years following the peace. Struggling to pay the massive war debt, German leaders printed more and more money and the money they printed became worth less and less. Both food and jobs were scarce. Before the country could recover economically, the Great Depression that paralyzed most of the world hit Germany as well, plunging it into even worse financial chaos.

THE POISONOUS MUSHROOM

An anti-Semitic picture book published in the 1930s was designed to teach children "what a danger the Jew is for the German folk and for the whole world." The book, *The Poisonous Mushroom* (in German, *Der Giftpilz*), which was used in some schools in Germany, contained seventeen stories depicting the Jew as "the Devil in human form." In the first story, "The Poisonous Mushroom," a mother uses the occasion of gathering mushrooms to instruct her young son. Just as there are edible mushrooms and poisonous ones, she explains, there are good people and deadly people. Her son already knows that the bad people are the Jews. The mother warns, "Just as a single poisonous mushroom can kill a whole family, so a solitary Jew can destroy a whole village, a whole city, even an entire folk."

By 1932, Germany was totally desolate. Foreign trade had dried up, banks had failed, and six million people were out of work. The empire that had spanned much of Europe was now a smaller, second-rate country; the once-revered monarchy was a squabbling government in disarray; and the greatest military on Earth was but a shadow of its former self. Many Germans, refusing to accept that their leaders' actions had set this chain of misery in motion, were willing to believe that the devastation was all the fault of the Jews.

AN ANGRY SOLDIER

One such man was Adolf Hitler. According to his autobiography, *Mein Kampf* (My Struggle), Hitler had made a conscious

Adolf Hitler is seen here in a 1921 photograph, shortly after joining the Nazi Party. His short stature and dark features contrast with his portrayal of the ideal German.

decision to be an anti-Semite early in his life. Although with his small frame, dark hair, and dark features, he looked nothing like the tall, blonde, blue-eyed Aryan he championed. He had a fanatical love for all things German. He was Austrian by birth, but he thought of himself as German by race and culture. He considered Jews to be of an inferior, alien race.

When the Great War started, Hitler received permission to fight for Germany. He was wounded twice in battle and received the Iron Cross for bravery. When he learned of Germany's surrender, he felt "indignation and disgrace," he later wrote in his autobiography. He burned with anger against the "miserable and degenerate criminals" who had ended the war, including Jews. The military defeat was the turning point that determined his career path. In *Mein Kampf*, he said that when the truce was signed, "my own fate became known to me. I decided to go into politics."

But politics was a demanding venture, and the thirty-year-old did not have much going for him. Although he read voraciously, he had dropped out of high school and therefore did not have an education. He had tried to become an artist but had little talent. Because he had drifted from job to job, he had no real work experience. He had no home, no family, no friends, and no connections. But he had one asset that was perfect for a political career: he was a great speaker.

A GIFTED ORATOR

Adolf Hitler could talk at length with passion and vigor. He could keep an audience spellbound for hours. It was not just his speaking style that drew crowds and worked them up; it was also that he told them what they wanted to hear. He extolled the glories of Germany, denounced the traitors who snatched victory from the army, and promised a restoration

In front of several microphones, Hitler speaks in his official capacity as chancellor, commander in chief, and Führer—absolute dictator of Germany.

of German honor. He railed against the Jews, declaring them to be at the root of every problem in German society.

Hitler's gift for oratory prompted the founder of the fledgling German Worker's Party to urge him to join the little group. His fiery speeches propelled him to the position of *Führer*, or leader, of the party in just two years. His ability to mesmerize crowds built the party from a handful of disgruntled rebels in 1919 to an army of 27,000 activists by 1925 and 178,000 in 1929. Hitler added the words "National Socialist" to the name "German Workers' Party" and the group became known by the shortened version of its first word (*Nazional*): the Nazi Party.

One of the goals of the Nazi Party was to overthrow the German government that had signed the Treaty of Versailles.

In November 1923, Hitler thought he had enough manpower to pull off such a coup. However, the plot, known as the Beer Hall Putsch (*Putsch* means "overthrow attempt"), was cut short by police, and Hitler and most of the other conspirators were arrested and tried for treason.

A SMALL STEP BACK AND A BIG LEAP FORWARD

What might have been a crushing blow to any other man Hitler turned into a springboard for fame. Before his arrest, his political ideas had been heard only in the city of Munich; his trial was a chance for a larger audience. Newsmen from all over the world would be covering the proceedings. For twenty-four days in the courtroom, Hitler commanded the spotlight. His eloquent defense of his revolutionary actions and his rants against Jews resonated with the German people who were dissatisfied with their plight and their government. When the trial was over, Hitler was found guilty of treason but admired by the masses.

Hitler spent only nine months of his five-year sentence in prison. He used that time to dictate his self-flattering autobiography to Rudolf Hess, a co-conspirator and fellow inmate. Anyone who read it would have noticed Hitler's twisted view of reality and his vicious anti-Semitism. Readers also would have got a glimpse of what he would do if he were in a position of power, for he speculated how much better Germany would be "if at the beginning of, or during, the war twelve thousand or fifteen thousand of these Jewish corrupters of the people had been plunged into an asphyxiating gas." Fifteen thousand was a small number compared with what he would actually have murdered.

CHAPTER 2

PREPARING THE FIRE: POLITICAL REVOLUTION

Hitler emerged from Landsberg Prison in 1924 with a new plan. His goal had not changed; he still wanted to lead a revolution. He wanted to overthrow the government and replace it with his own version of a glorious Reich—an empire that stretched across Europe, was void of all Jews, and answered to him as absolute ruler. Now, however, he had a new strategy for achieving his goal. Instead of armed rebellion, he would work within the law. He would build his party's strength to the point where he could gain control of the government legitimately.

BUILDING THE PARTY

Hitler's speeches had attracted a number of former soldiers and others unable to find jobs in the struggling economy, and Hitler made use of them. Postwar politics in Germany was a rowdy business of angry debates conducted in beer halls and open-air meetings. Dozens of political groups tried to out-argue or outshout one another, and scuffles were common. Hitler organized the volunteers who came to him

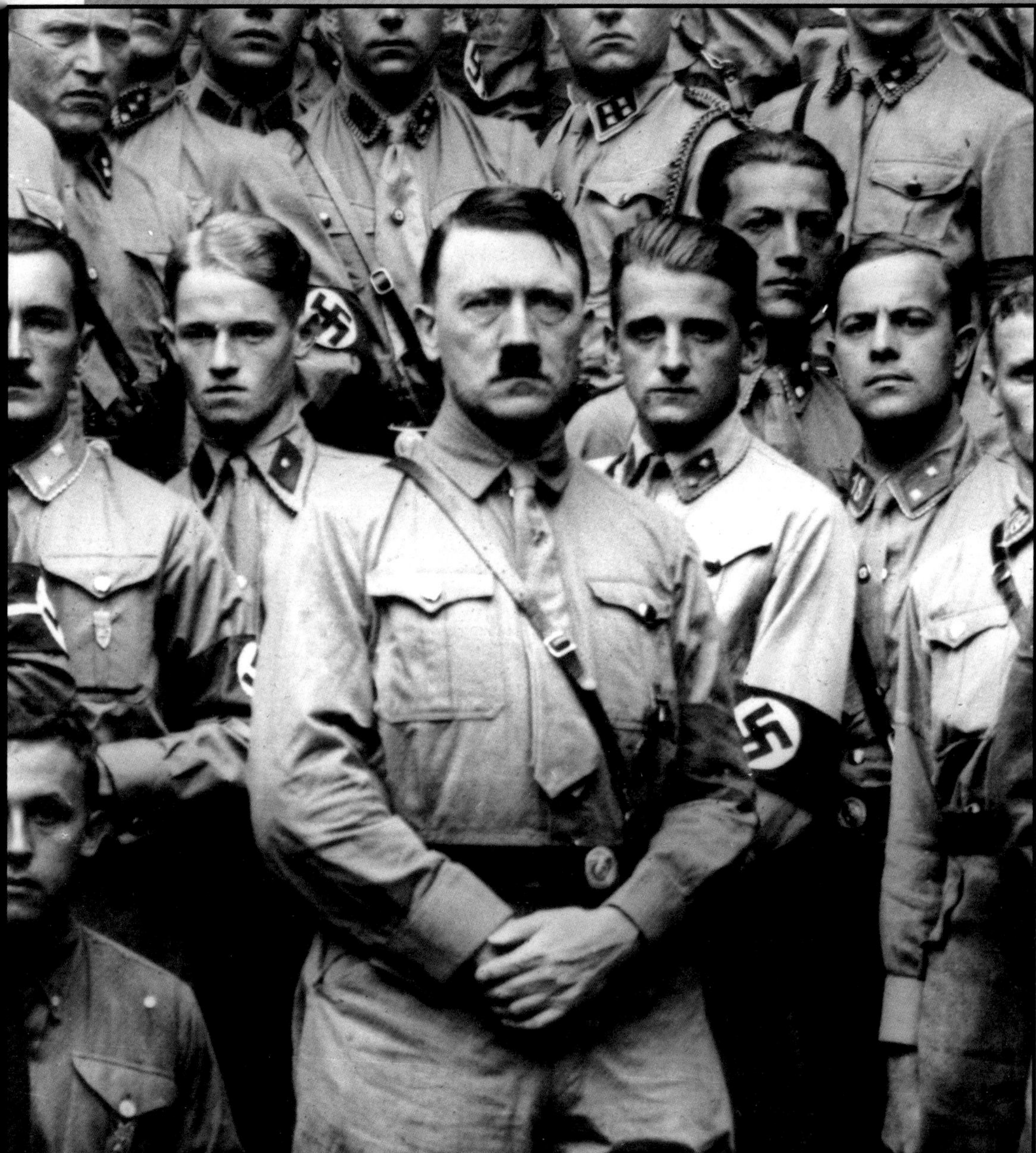

Hitler poses with his elite military group, the SS. Their name, Schutzstaffel, means "protection squad." They pledged their loyalty not to Germany, but to Hitler.

into a military-like squad of thugs who kept order at Nazi meetings and disrupted the gatherings of other parties. He called them the *Sturmabteilung* (SA), or "Storm Troops." They were also called "Brownshirts" because of the color of their uniforms.

From this growing band of soldiers, Hitler selected the most disciplined and most brutal to serve as his personal bodyguards. He put them in black uniforms instead of brown; they were the Black Guard, the *Schutzstaffel* (SS). Over the next several years, the SS grew larger, stronger, and more ruthless and the "Blackshirts" eventually replaced the Brownshirts.

At first, however, it was the Storm Troops that led the demonstrations Hitler staged to gather support for his cause. They marched with goose steps beneath a banner Hitler had designed: a black swastika on a white circle against a red background. No one within earshot of one of the rallies could mistake the Nazis' goals. A leader would call out loudly, "Germany!" and the soldiers would reply, "Awake!" Then the leader would yell, "Jews!" The response: "Die!"

Hitler needed the Nazi Party to be more than a collection of marchers and shouters—it had to be able to replace the government when the time was right. A master at organization, Hitler set up Nazi agencies that mirrored government structures: departments of agriculture, labor, economy, justice, and so forth. It even had a department of foreign affairs. Hitler instilled party loyalty by creating Nazi groups for every interest; there were doctor, lawyer, teacher, student, and artist groups and Nazi clubs for women, youths, and children.

The Nazi Party was basically a government, much like a country. In fact, in some ways the party was stronger than the nation of Germany. The Treaty of Versailles limited Germany's army to one hundred thousand men; Hitler's

Hitler waves to crowds along a parade route in 1933. He has just been named chancellor, and he shares a car with German president Paul von Hindenburg.

Storm Troops numbered four hundred thousand in 1932 and eventually exceeded four million.

GAINING POWER

With the Storm Troops intimidating and attacking Hitler's opponents on the streets, the growing enthusiasm for the Nazi Party, and Hitler's untiring campaigning and speaking, the Nazi Party began to win elections. When the Great

Depression put six million Germans out of work in 1930, Hitler jumped on the opportunity to blame the Jews and paint his party as the hope for a brighter future. As a result, every two years beginning in 1928, more and more Nazis were elected to the Reichstag, the German legislature. In 1932, the Nazi Party won 230 of the Reichstag's 491 seats.

The Nazis held more seats than any other faction, with the Communists in second place and a few smaller groups

THE NIGHT OF THE LONG KNIVES

As merciless as Hitler was to the Jews, he was equally cruel to any who opposed him. Ernst Röhm had been Hitler's friend and faithful ally for fourteen years, since joining the Nazi Party in 1919. He had stood with him in the Beer Hall Putsch and gone to prison. He had rebuilt the SA into a ruthless army at Hitler's request. After Hitler became chancellor, Röhm pushed to continue the revolution Hitler had begun. He wanted to incorporate the German army into his SA and crush all conservatives. Some of the other Nazi leaders feared that Röhm was becoming too powerful. Disagreements and distrust were rampant in the party ranks, and some influential Nazis accused Röhm of wanting to overthrow Hitler. Hitler had to choose between his friend and the people who could keep him in power. In a bloody purge that foreshadowed the way Hitler would rule, the SS descended on a meeting of SA leaders and the homes of totally unrelated opponents of Hitler. When the long night ended, at least 150 to 200 people were dead, perhaps as many as 1,000. An additional thousand were imprisoned. The SA declined in power and the SS rose. Historians call the treacherous spree the Night of the Long Knives, after a legend from British medieval history. Röhm, still loyal to the man who ordered his assassination, was reported to have died uttering the words, "Heil, Hitler!"

behind them. But no party had a majority. So the president, Paul von Hindenburg, needed to select a chancellor. The chancellor's job was to lead the cabinet, the heads of the different government departments. After some political maneuvering among several men who wanted the position, Hindenburg reluctantly appointed Hitler to the post on January 30, 1933.

But being chancellor of Germany was not enough for Hitler. He could not carry out all his revolutionary ideas unless he alone had control. He needed to get rid of his political rivals, especially the Communists. He set about reducing their influence using the tactics that were the standards of his rule: deception and violence.

On the night of February 27, 1933, the Reichstag building, the symbol of German government, was intentionally set on fire. The police arrested a suspicious man, a not-too-bright Dutch Communist who just "happened" to be in the area, and Hitler immediately blamed the incident on Communists. The very next day, he persuaded President Hindenburg to sign an emergency decree that abolished many personal freedoms and made it easy for him to arrest people who opposed him. In fact, in the weeks after the Reichstag fire, more than four thousand of the political enemies of the Nazis were arrested.

SEIZING CONTROL

Hitler prepared to arrest even more. A munitions factory in the town of Dachau outside Munich was quickly transformed into a prison. However, it was not called a prison; careful use of words was part of Nazi deception. The press release announcing its opening called it "the first concentration camp," the place where "all Communist . . . and Social

Political prisoners at a factory in Dachau that will become a concentration camp are building living quarters for the SS who will be stationed there as guards.

Democrat functionaries who endanger state security will be interned together"—that is, concentrated in one location. The camp was opened March 22, 1933, just in time for Hitler's next move.

That move, the very next day, was to coerce the Reichstag to pass the Enabling Act, a law that would give Hitler's cabinet—instead of the Reichstag—the sole and complete authority to make laws. Such a sweeping change required a "yes" from three-fourths of the Reichstag's members present for the vote, and Hitler did not have that many "yeses." So he made sure that some of the people who would vote "no" were

Seventeen days after the death of President Hindenburg, smiling Germans vote to approve Hitler's ascension to power as head of Germany, greeting him with the Nazi salute.

absent when the vote was taken. They were either arrested or intimidated by the SA into staying away. The vote was 84 percent in favor of giving Hitler total control over making laws for Germany.

The Enabling Act gave Hitler that control for only four years, and he could not risk a future Reichstag taking away his power. So he made a new law that declared that the Nazi Party was the only political party permitted in Germany.

Now all that stood in his way of absolute rule was the eighty-seven-year-old president. That barrier was removed on August 4, 1934, when Hindenburg died. Hitler informed the people that, on the previous day, the cabinet had approved a law combining the offices of chancellor and president. That meant that Hitler was in charge of not only the legislature, but also the executive branch and the army. He claimed for himself the title not only of chancellor, but also of Führer. He immediately made every soldier swear an oath to "render unconditional obedience" not to Germany, but "to Adolf Hitler, the Führer of the German Reich and people, Supreme Commander of the Armed Forces."

Thus, in only nineteen months, he had achieved the revolution he described in *Mein Kampf.* He had transformed Germany from a constitutional republic to a one-party dictatorship. He had advanced from a man on probation for treason to the absolute dictator of more than sixty-five million people. Of that number, more than half a million were Jews.

CHAPTER 3

SPARKS BEGIN: EXCLUSION

Before Hitler rose to power, anti-Semitism in Germany was somewhat limited to speech makers and people who wrote books and pamphlets. Many Germans might have believed the propaganda of the Jew haters, but they did not let it affect their daily lives. Once Hitler was in office, however, attitudes toward Jews took an ugly turn. In speech after speech, the Führer branded Jews the enemies of the nation, and people equated dislike of Jews with patriotism. Prejudice turned into persecution. In an interview with the U.S. Holocaust Memorial Museum, one woman recalled what the change was like for a girl of eight:

> **[Before Hitler came to power,] I had lots of German friends. I had little kids who played with me, and went to school with me. ...But it changed, it changed in 1933. It changed a lot. ...One girl...we played together, and at one point she said to me, "You know, Carola, I can't play with you anymore."**
> **And I said, "How come?"**
> **She said, "Because you're a Jew."**

I said, "What is that?"
She said, "Well, have you heard of Hitler?"
I said, "Yes" because every morning they used to say "Heil, Hitler."..."But why can't you play with me anymore? Why?"
She said, "Because my father told me that you're Jewish, and Gentile children, Aryan kids, can no longer play with the Jewish kids."

PERSECUTION STARTS YOUNG

The antagonism between Aryan children and Jewish children after 1933 was reinforced in the schools. Even very young students were separated in their classrooms; non-Aryan students had to sit in the "Jew corner" and play apart from their Aryan classmates in the schoolyard. Jewish students could not compete in sports or other activities. They were teased and called dreadful names, sometimes by teachers as well as other children.

Peter Prager described to the Shoah Foundation his experience as a child of ten. The school year began in April, but the year Hitler was appointed chancellor, the start of classes was delayed until the head teacher could be replaced by a Nazi and several "unreliable" teachers could be dismissed. Prager remembered the Nazi salute being required before each class and Saturday lessons on the history of the Nazi Party. Only three Jewish students were in his class, and they were permitted only because their fathers had fought in the Great War. Worst of all were the racial lessons. Prager recalled them vividly:

We had a professor of biology. We went to the classroom. There were all around us

PERSECUTION ON PAUSE

For two short weeks, Jews in Berlin relaxed a little. The anti-Semitic signs had been removed. The newspapers and magazines had toned down their attacks against them. Even the police had stopped their taunting. The reason? The eleventh Olympiad.

Germany had been awarded the venue for the 1936 Summer Olympics five years earlier. At that time the move was seen as welcoming the vanquished aggressor of the Great War back into the family of peaceful nations. But by the time the games actually started, Adolf Hitler had brought many changes to Germany. He had ejected Jews from all sports, and Jewish organizations urged athletes worldwide to boycott the Olympics in Berlin. But failing to realize or admit the seriousness of Nazi anti-Semitism, forty-nine nations chose to participate in the games.

Hitler used the Olympics to promote his idea that Aryans were physically superior to all other people. Germany won more medals than any other country, but the Führer was publicly embarrassed when the African American Jesse Owens was the event's top athlete, the first person ever to take home four gold medals.

When the games ended, the "No Jews Allowed" posters went back up. Newspapers resumed their rants, and police grew stern again. But for two weeks in 1936, Berlin's Jews could walk the streets freely and shop wherever they wished.

pictures of heads of people. One of them was Hindenburg, his head. And he said that these were all Germanic heads; and now Jewish heads are different. And then he asked us three Jews to stand up. And I had to come to the front. He measured me with

While a Jewish family walks the streets of a German city in 1933, a group of Storm Troops laughs and yells insults at them.

a tape measure. Measured me to show this is so many centimeters short. He said to me, "Don't worry, I'm not doing to you any harm. It's not your fault that you're Jewish. But that shows inferiority.

Parents were powerless to protect their children from such ridicule. They were victims of discrimination as well. Some Germans refused to do business with stores that were owned by Jews, and many shops and restaurants posted "Jews Not Welcome" signs. In some places, park benches or entire parks were off limits to Jews. Some cities had "No Jews Allowed" placards at their entrances. A number of doctors turned away Jewish patients.

The Storm Troops, always eager for an excuse to flex their muscles, delighted in taunting Jews wherever they found them. They bullied or beat innocent citizens and sometimes carted them off to jail on trumped-up charges. For example, when a Jewish lawyer asked the Munich police to help a client when a mob broke out the windows of his store, the police permitted the Brownshirts to beat the lawyer savagely, knocking out teeth and puncturing his eardrum. The SA shaved his head, cut off his pant legs at the knees, and paraded him through the city, barefoot and bleeding. He had to carry a sign that read, "I will never again complain to the police."

PERSECUTION IN THE MARKETPLACE

The mistreatment of the Jews of Germany, particularly the vicious attacks by the Storm Troops, was reported in other countries. Outraged people in the United States, England, France, and other places threatened to boycott products that came from Germany. Hitler saw this action as an opportunity to inflict even more damage on his enemy. He accused the Jews of spreading false rumors about the Nazis "in order to incite world opinion against Germany," according to posters plastered on the streets. The posters called for Germans to "defend themselves against this criminal slander" by boycotting all Jewish businesses.

The posters went up on March 29, 1933, announcing that the boycott would begin April 1. On the morning of the first, the Brownshirts fanned out in the major cities, painting the Star of David, the international symbol of Jews, or the word "Jew" on stores, offices, and shops owned by Jews.

As this woman reads the sign Nazi Storm Troops posted in the window of this shoe store, she must decide whether to go along with the boycott of Jewish businesses.

They planted themselves in front of the businesses, in their intimidating uniforms, and held signs warning Aryans not to enter.

Many Germans ignored the signs and shopped in the targeted stores. Many others not only boycotted the businesses, but also vandalized the buildings. Some physically attacked store owners and other Jews. The boycott was the first official act in Hitler's war against the Jews.

PERSECUTION MADE LEGAL

The next acts came swiftly. One week after the boycott, the government issued the first of a series of laws excluding Jews from all public institutions. By the end of April, Jews could not hold any government job, Jewish doctors could not work in government hospitals, Jews could not serve on juries, and non-Aryans could number no more than 1.5 percent of the total number of students in a public school.

A problem with these laws, from the Nazi viewpoint, was that some people might be able to get around them by concealing or neglecting to reveal that they were Jewish. To close that loophole, two new laws were passed: the Law for the Protection of German Blood and German Honor and the Reich Citizenship Law. Notice of these laws was announced at a Nazi Party rally in the city of Nuremberg in September 1935. The measures, together with several supplementary decrees that expanded them, became known as the Nuremberg Race Laws. They defined very precisely what made a person a Jew: anyone with three Jewish grandparents was a Jew no matter what religious beliefs that person had, if any. Thus hundreds of people who had never practiced Judaism—some who were lifelong Christians—were classified as Jewish overnight.

Thousands listen as Hitler addresses the annual convention of the Nazi Party in Nuremberg in 1935, where the racial laws denying Jews citizenship were announced.

The first Nuremberg Law forbade Jews from marrying or having sexual relations with Aryans. It also said Jews could not employ female Aryans who were under the age of forty-five as servants in their homes and prohibited Jews from flying the German flag. The second law, the Reich Citizenship Law, declared that Jews were subjects of Germany, but they were not German citizens.

The Nuremberg Laws made the next spate of legislation much simpler for Hitler. By making regulations that limited various activities to citizens, he could put every facet of German life out of reach of every Jew. That is exactly what he did. Over the next few months and years, Jews were excluded from universities and dismissed from other schools; barred from working as doctors, dentists, and lawyers; not allowed to perform as actors; and banned from journalism,

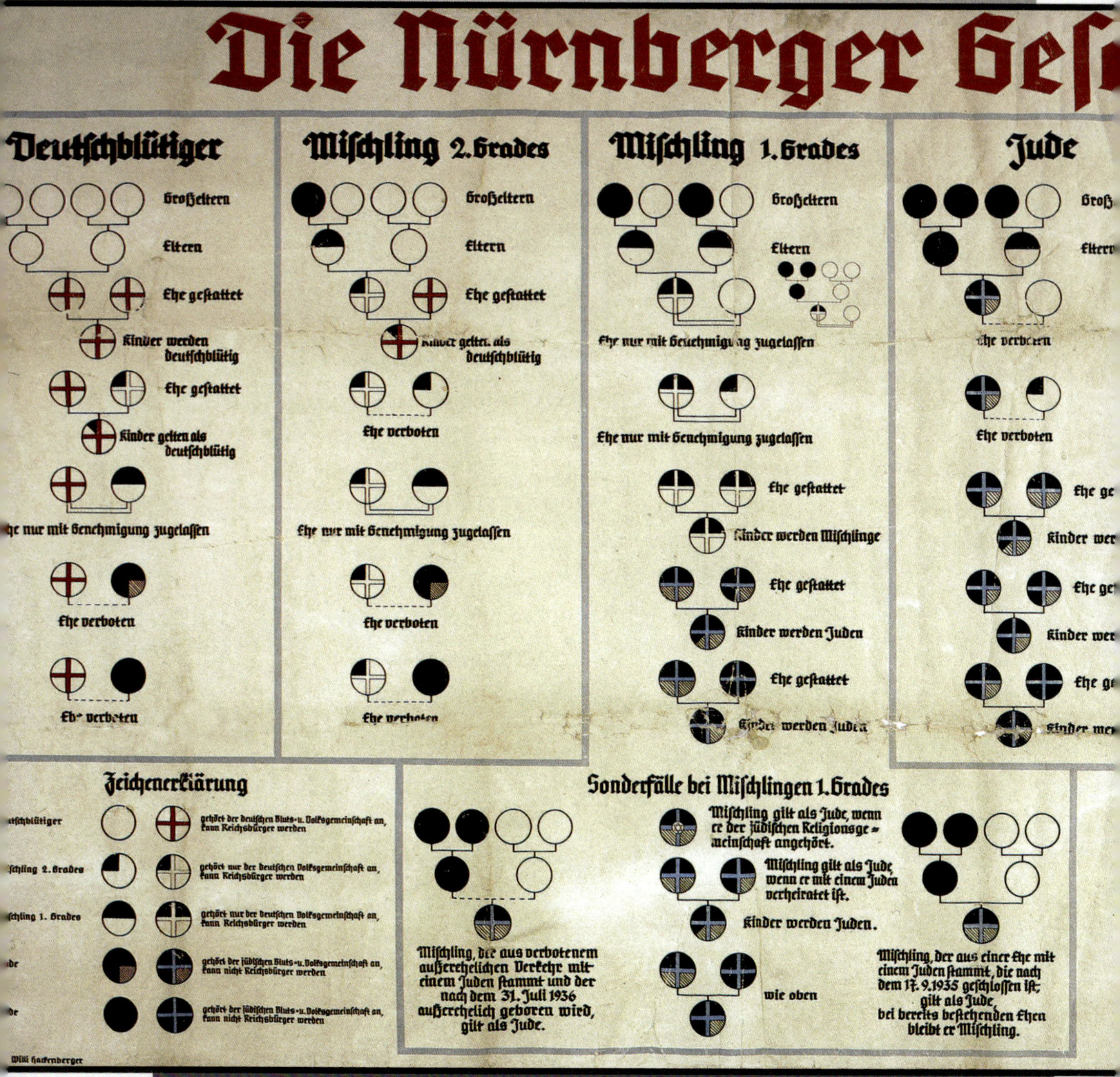

This Nazi chart was an attempt to explain the Nuremberg race laws. Non-Jews were represented by white circles and Jews by black circles. Various levels of "part Jews" are depicted.

farming, radio, and the stock exchange. Opera houses, theaters, and sports facilities were closed to Jews, as were "Aryan zones" in some cities.

"SUBTLE" PERSUASION

The many anti-Semitic laws had one purpose: convince the Jews to leave Germany voluntarily. The tactic worked to a point. In the first year of Nazi rule, thirty-seven thousand Jews fled the country. But more than four hundred thousand remained. Hitler tried a new strategy: taking over Jewish businesses.

Before 1933, Jews owned one hundred thousand businesses in Germany, including fifty thousand stores. The April 1 boycott was the first attempt to destroy those enterprises. A media campaign that equated refusing to buy from Jews with patriotism, together with armed harassment at the doors of shops and offices, ate into Jewish profits. Many Jews had no choice but to sell their businesses to non-Jews at a fraction of their worth. This forced transfer of Jewish to Aryan German ownership of businesses was called Aryanization. By 1938, Jews owned only nine thousand stores in the entire country, less than 20 percent of the number owned when the Nazi terror began. By that year, the exclusion of Jews from German life was nearly complete.

CHAPTER 4

THE TORCH IS LIT: KRISTALLNACHT

How did the Jews cope? They turned to one another. Each city had its own *kehilla*, a traditional Jewish organization that met the needs of the community. The kehilla tried to provide whatever the Nazis took away. The Nazis expelled Jewish children from schools; the kehilla set up its own schools. The Nazis burned books by Jewish authors; the kehilla established publishing houses. The Nazis barred Jews from the arts; the kehilla organized plays, concerts, and art exhibits. The kehilla fed Jews who had no jobs, lent them money, and helped them start new businesses in the Jewish community.

Why didn't more Jews leave Germany? Most did not recognize the danger. Even though the restrictions were harsh, periods of intense persecution were followed by weeks or months of relative calm. Many thought they could weather the storm. Holocaust survivor Ruth Drescher, in a speech at Seton Hill University, recalled her father's attitude: "Leave Germany? How could I do that? This is my home. I fought in the war…We will be safe here. This Hitler business will pass."

NOWHERE TO GO

But the persecution did not pass; it grew harsher. Hitler's goal of having his Reich *Judenrein*—free or "cleansed" of Jews—through voluntary emigration was not being accomplished quickly enough. The Nazis needed to push the Jews out. The forced expulsions began after Germany took over Austria in March 1938. That annexation added two hundred thousand Jews to the territory Hitler controlled. The Führer sent Adolf Eichmann to Austria with instructions to cleanse it of Jews.

On May 10, 1933, university students in thirty-four cities across Germany held rallies like this one in Berlin and burned more than twenty-five thousand "un-German" books.

Eichmann's methods were the same as Hitler's: deception and violence. When he could not trick or intimidate Jews into leaving, he Aryanized their property and possessions. He used money from the Aryanization to finance the removal of those who would not leave. In Eichmann's first eight months, more than one hundred thousand Jews left Austria.

Among the Jews to flee Nazi Germany before Kristallnacht were Albert Einstein (*left*) and movie director Ernst Lubitsch. They are pictured here in Palm Springs, California.

But ridding Germany and the lands it acquired of Jews became increasingly difficult. Where could so many people go? Most went to nearby countries, where they were again trapped when Germany invaded its neighbors. Many applied for entry to nations far from the widening Nazi net, and in July 1938, world leaders held a conference in Evian, France, to consider how to respond to the growing crisis. Most nations had limits on the number of immigrants they would receive from any one country. The U.S. quota for Germany and Austria combined was twenty-seven thousand per year, far below the three hundred thousand who sought U.S. visas. Of the thirty-two countries represented at Evian, only the Dominican Republic offered to accept Jewish refugees; all the others kept their doors tightly shut.

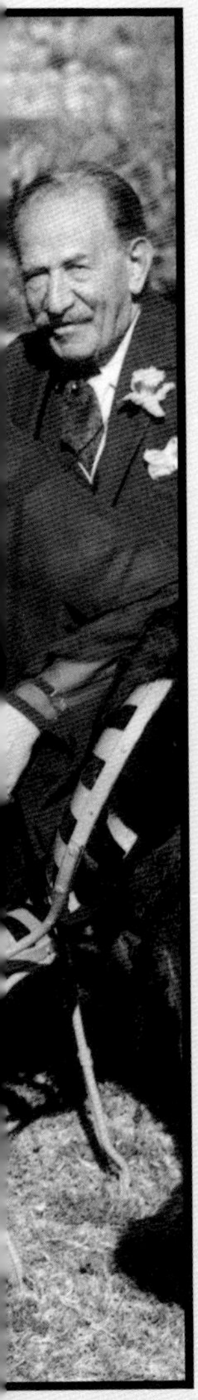

A RACE AGAINST THE CLOCK

Hitler did not let the actions of other countries stop him in his determination to make Germany *Judenrein*. On October 6, 1938, Poland gave notice that all Polish passports would expire at the end of the month. No Poles living outside Poland could return after October unless they revalidated their passports before they expired. Fifty thousand Polish Jews lived in Germany and Austria—Jews Hitler wanted returned to Poland. Scrambling to meet the deadline, the Gestapo (the state police) rounded up seventeen thousand Polish Jews on October 28 and dumped them at the Polish border. Twenty-three years later, at the trial of Adolf Eichmann, Zindel Grynszpan described the sudden nightmare:

At eight o'clock a policeman came in. "You will come to the 11th precinct—with the

After they took over Austria, the Nazis tormented Jews by forcing them to do humiliating tasks, such as scrubbing streets. They sometimes made rabbis use their prayer shawls as rags.

passports . . . no need to take anything with you." Then we were taken . . . old people, small children, and someone shouting: "Sign! The deportation order! You are being deported!" . . . And then they loaded us onto the police vans . . . and we were dispatched to the railway station; the streets were black with people [shouting] "Out with the Jews! Go to Palestine!" We were taken by train to. . . the German-Polish border.

THE WHITE ROSE

Not everyone in Germany ignored the suffering of the Jews. Two college students, Hans and Sophie Scholl, were disgusted when they saw Nazis belittling and tormenting Jews on the streets of Munich. When they heard from the pulpit of their church how the persecution had turned into mass murder, they decided they would do what they could to stop it. Most Germans did not know what was going on in the far reaches of the Reich. The Scholls were determined to get this information to the public.

Enlisting the help of three other students and one professor, they formed the White Rose resistance group. They made copies of the sermon that had inspired them and secretly placed them all over their campus. They printed five additional leaflets declaring that it was "the holiest duty of every German to destroy these [Nazi] beasts."

Other students in other cities took up the group's cause. They reprinted the fliers and distributed them in their areas. Before long the "leaves of the White Rose" could be found all over Germany and Austria. But merely possessing, much less creating, such material was illegal in Nazi Germany, punishable by death. Sophie was caught with the pamphlets and all six members of the group were arrested and convicted of treason. As the guillotine fell, Hans proclaimed, "Long live freedom!"

. . . Each of us was searched to see whether any of us had any money with him; one could not have more than ten marks. . . They told us we would now walk 2 kilometers [1.2 miles] to the Polish border. . . The SS started whipping us over the heads, hitting us. Those who fell behind, those unable to

> **walk, were dragged on the road; blood was flowing on all sides. The bundles we had in our hands were torn away from us and thrown aside. They acted most barbarically.**

One day Grynszpan was operating a store in Hanover, Germany; two days later he, his wife, and two of their children were penniless refugees in Zbąszyń, Poland. One of his sons, seventeen-year-old Herschel, was living in Paris, France. Herschel's sister wanted him to know where to contact the family, so she mailed him a note. In it she gave a brief description of their ordeal.

THE SPARK THAT BEGAN THE HOLOCAUST

What could a seventeen-year-old in France do for his family in the no-man's land between Germany and Poland? What power did one young man have against an armed nation? Perhaps in his frustration, revenge was the only answer that came to Herschel. He purchased a revolver, took a train to the German embassy in Paris, and asked to see a German official. When a junior diplomat, Ernst vom Rath, responded, Herschel shot him; he died two days later.

The young assassin waited calmly for the French police to arrest him. In his pocket was a letter explaining his actions to his parents: "I could not do otherwise, may God forgive me, the heart bleeds when I hear of your tragedy and that of the twelve thousand Jews [deported with you]. I

Herschel Grynszpan covers his face as French policemen lead him to a courtroom. He was eventually imprisoned in Germany until at least 1942, but his final fate is unknown.

must protest so that the whole world hears my protest, and that I will do. Forgive me."

Herschel Grynszpan's loud protest was a godsend for Hitler. It was the excuse he needed to terrorize the Jews and blame the savagery on them. It was the spark he needed to ignite his war against the Jews. On the night vom Rath died, the Führer ordered a pogrom, a vicious coordinated assault against Jewish lives and property throughout his domain.

But in keeping with his use of deception in everything he did, the attacks had to look like the spontaneous actions of ordinary citizens—Germans' reaction to the Jewish assassination of the diplomat. The Brownshirts and Hitler Youth would carry out the destruction, but they would need to dress in plainclothes. They would wield clubs, axes, hammers, and torches, rather than rifles or bayonets. The outbursts would have to occur at the same time in cities throughout the country so that central coordination would not be obvious.

DECEPTION AND DESTRUCTION

At 1:20 AM on October 10, 1938, Reinhard Heydrich, who was in charge of the Security Police of the Reich, sent a "most urgent telegram" to police forces all over Germany. He informed them that "following the attempt on the life of Secretary of the Legation vom Rath in Paris, demonstrations against the Jews are to be expected in all parts of the Reich in the course of the coming night, November 9/10, 1938." He issued these instructions, as reported on the Jewish Virtual Library's website:

> **The Chiefs of the State Police, or their deputies, must immediately upon receipt of this telegram contact, by telephone, the political leaders in their areas...to discuss**

Germans had to clear glass from the streets after Kristallnacht. Insurance companies calculated the cost of replacing the windows at five million reichsmarks ($1.25 million).

> **the arrangements for the demonstrations... Synagogues are to be burned down only where there is no danger of fire in neighboring buildings. ...Places of business and apartments belonging to Jews may be destroyed but not looted. ...Particular care is to be taken that non-Jewish businesses are completely protected against damage. ...The demonstrations are not to be prevented by the Police. ...As soon as the course of events during the night permits, ...as many Jews in all districts—especially the rich—as can be accommodated in existing prisons are to be arrested. For the time being only healthy male Jews, who are not too old, are to be detained. After the detentions have been carried out the appropriate concentration camps are to be contacted immediately for the prompt accommodation of the Jews in the camps.**

All through the night of the ninth and long into the tenth, the professional mobs tore through hundreds of cities, towns, and villages, hacking, slashing, and burning as they went. The sound of thousands of windows shattering gave a name to this orgy of mayhem and devastation: *Kristallnacht*, the Night of Broken Glass.

BURNED AND BROKEN

Among the targets of the Storm Troops were the symbols of Judaism: the synagogues, Jewish houses of worship. In an

Firemen try to keep a building from burning as fire destroys the Prinzregenten Street synagogue in the background, one of seven synagogues set on fire in Berlin on Kristallnacht.

interview with the Wisconsin Historical Society, Rabbi Manfred Swarsensky described some of what he saw in Berlin:

> **At about two o'clock in the morning...the telephone rang and...the resident sexton of the Synagogue Prinzregentstrasse called me and shouted over the phone, "Our synagogue is burning!"**
>
> **Then, I got up, ran to the synagogue, pushed my hat way down in my face so as not to be recognized by anyone, and there I saw German SS troopers pour gasoline into the interior of the building and over the walls, and also German firemen stand on adjoining building so as to prevent that they be burnt down and so they poured water over those buildings so as to keep them cool so to speak.**
>
> **And then I ran, closer toward dawn, to the other synagogue, which was not too far. The Fasanenstrasse Synagogue, which at one time the Kaiser had visited...And there I saw the same picture, three huge domes... and the fire rising from the pews up into the cupolas [domes], and a horrible sight.**

Thirteen hundred synagogues were burned that night; an additional seventy-six that could not be burned without damaging other buildings were destroyed by other means. Holy books and scrolls were ripped apart and sacred items torn and trampled.

The synagogues were symbolic targets for the vandals. The real targets, the buildings that could cripple the Jews economically, were their stores and other businesses. They had been clearly marked months before during the April boycott, so the Brownshirts and Hitler Youth had no trouble identifying them. Ignoring the shops of Aryans, they took sledgehammers, crowbars, and bricks to the windows of buildings belonging to Jews. Disregarding Heydrich's prohibition against looting, they left the merchandise behind the broken glass to the mercy of the towns' citizens who followed in their wake. The official government report said 815 shops had been destroyed, but Heydrich put the number at 7,500.

BROKEN PEOPLE

The Nazis did not stop with synagogues and stores; they went after individuals in their homes. The experience that twelve-year-old Rita Braumann of Cologne related to Holocaust researcher Martin Gilbert was typical:

> **The noise was terrifying. ...Absolutely everything had been demolished. Shattered glass made it dangerous to walk anywhere. Bottles of wine had been poured over Persian carpets, home-made jam had been emptied all over the place...valuable paintings had been slashed with an axe or knives.**

In some homes, the heartbreak was far greater than a matter of broken furniture and sliced artwork. According to the official accounting, 171 houses were burned during the riot. Even destroyed homes were not the worst of it. Laurie Lowenthal told Martin Gilbert what happened to his family in Aschaffenburg:

> **We were woken by the sound of shooting. My father's cousin...lived on the first floor**

> **of our house with his family. Two men broke down their front door and shot him point blank while he was in bed. ...His brother-in-law...was kidnapped, taken to the nearby woods, tied to a tree and used as target practice.**

Before the rampage was over, ninety-one Jews were dead and thirty-six seriously wounded. Thirty thousand Jewish men had been arrested and taken to concentration camps at Dachau, Sachsenhausen, and Buchenwald. The savage cruelty of Hitler's war against the Jews was no longer masked. Kristallnacht marked a decisive point in that war. From that moment on, Jews would have no rights, no protections, and no possessions. Brutality would be part of the persecution. Killing Jews was officially sanctioned. The events of November 9–10, 1938, were the first steps in Hitler's plan, announced years earlier in *Mein Kampf*, to totally annihilate the Jews.

CHAPTER 5

THE FIRE BLAZES: THE HOLOCAUST

The immediate aftermath of Kristallnacht was horrendous. The financial cost alone was staggering. The insurance companies estimated that replacing just the broken windows would come to five million marks, and the total cost was likely to be three times that amount. Most of the damaged buildings, although they housed Jewish shops, were owned by Aryans. To the Nazis, the solution was simple: make the Jews foot the bill. Accordingly, a fine of one billion marks ($400 million in 1938) was levied against the Jewish community.

How could the Reich exact such an exorbitant sum from people whose livelihoods had just been smashed to pieces? It could take what was left of their possessions. Two days after the fury began to subside, on November 12, 1938, Nazi officials issued the Decree on the Exclusion of Jews from German Economic Life. As the title plainly indicates, the purpose of the edict was to shut Jews out of all buying and selling in Germany. Jewish businesses were to be transferred to Aryans. In a matter of weeks, a flurry of laws confiscated gold and silver, stocks and bonds, and jewelry and artwork owned by Jews; prohibited Jews from working in any of the professions; banned Jews from owning any type of weapon; took cars and driver's licenses away from Jews; expelled any Jews still in German schools; and imposed a curfew on Jews.

THE HUMAN COST

The financial cost of Kristallnacht was enormous, but the human toll was chilling. Most of the thirty thousand dragged to concentration camps were released within months if they

These are some of the ten thousand Jewish men imprisoned in the Buchenwald concentration camp immediately after Kristallnacht. Their heads are shaved to prevent the possibility of lice infestation.

promised they would leave Germany. But they came home broken in body as well as spirit. Few would talk about the tortures they saw and experienced.

But some of the men did not come home. At that time, the Nazis were concerned about how the rest of the world viewed Germany; they did not want to be accused of mistreating their prisoners. So any death in the concentration camps was passed off as having resulted from natural causes. Ursula Rosenfeld, like many others, believed the lie until other Jews returned to her small town. She told an interviewer for the book and movie *Into the Arms of Strangers* (2000) what had happened to her father:

> **When they came to Buchenwald and they took away all the men's braces [suspenders] and shoelaces, [my father] protested and said, "You can't treat old people like this." So they made an example of him and they beat him to death in front of everybody in order to instill terror and obedience. We heard a few days later that he had died of a heart attack, but this was the story the Nazis told all the families of the people they killed. We learned the true story later from people who were released from Buchenwald.**

THE WORLD IS SILENT

The Nazis were quick to throw the blame off themselves for the terrible destruction. The government-controlled newspaper in Berlin portrayed the pogrom as a thoroughly justified reaction of the Aryan citizens to a Jewish crime:

> **The announcement of the decease of the diplomat and party member vom Rath by the cowardly hand of the Jewish murderer has aroused spontaneous anti-Jewish demonstrations throughout the Reich. The German Peoples' profound indignation has given vent to powerful anti-Jewish activities.**

The news report falsely praised the restraint of the people: "Shop windows have been smashed and the show-cases of Jewish shopkeepers wrecked, [but] the goods themselves remained untouched… Not one finger was laid on the Jews themselves."

However, foreign correspondents stationed in Germany got the real story out to people in their countries. World opinion was stirred by the atrocities, but only briefly. No nation was outraged enough to do anything to help the Jews. U.S. president Franklin Roosevelt recalled the American ambassador to Germany and extended the visas of German refugees who had managed to make it to the United States, but those actions were of no help to the thousands trapped among people

Americans in New York City, outraged over the events of Kristallnacht, protest the actions of the Nazis and praise President Franklin Roosevelt's decision to recall the U.S. ambassador to Germany.

bent on their destruction. People in America were more concerned with keeping out immigrants than helping foreigners.

People reading the newspapers might have thought the reports were exaggerated. They might have assumed that the incident was an aberration, a departure from normal life in Germany. They might have imagined, as many German Jews once did, that the "Hitler business" would pass and could therefore be ignored. In all probability, no one at the time foresaw the murderous extent to which Hitler would go

NO PORT IN THE STORM

The 937 refugees, nearly all Jewish, were relieved to be leaving Germany. They had applied for entry into the United States, but they didn't have time to wait for the visas. They all had Cuban landing certificates and transit visas that allowed them to land in Cuba and wait there until their U.S. visas came through. They set sail on the German liner *St. Louis* on May 13, 1939, with high hopes.

None of them knew that a week before the ship left Hamburg, the Cuban government had cancelled all landing certificates; only a few passengers who had U.S. visas were permitted to get off the boat in Cuba. The ship tried to dock in Miami, but the United States refused its request. The discouraged refugees were forced to return to Europe. Steering clear of Germany, the passengers were finally accepted by England, France, Belgium, and the Netherlands. More than half of the refugees on the *St. Louis*—532—ended up in lands that were taken over by Nazi forces.

in his hatred of Jews. Whatever the reasons, the world was largely silent.

LIGHTS IN THE DARKNESS

However, a few voices rose to denounce the injustice, and brave people acted to ease the fear and suffering of the Jews. In the Netherlands, a Committee for Special Jewish Affairs was established in 1933 to provide food, housing, and emotional support for the Jews who crossed the Dutch border to find refuge. In France, the Children's Aid Society set up homes for Jewish children who escaped from Germany; some had been orphaned by the Nazi pogrom and others were sent by desperate parents to what they hoped was safety.

Probably the brightest light in the dark days following Kristallnacht shone in England. A number of groups there joined forces to devise a plan that would enable children to escape the brutality. Along with nearly every other country, England had closed its doors to large numbers of immigrants, but the Refugee Children's Movement convinced the British government to allow children to come to England for brief stays. They would remain only until the persecution ended, then they would return. The Nazis, eager to rid Germany of its Jews, agreed.

The program, known as the Kindertransport (*Kinder* is German for "children") was a massive undertaking. The rescue groups had to find sponsors who would adopt the children temporarily, figure out how to choose which children could participate, arrange transportation, and raise private funds to pay for it all. The English people rose to the challenge, and in the nine months Germany permitted the transports, ten thousand children were rescued from the flames that consumed most of their parents.

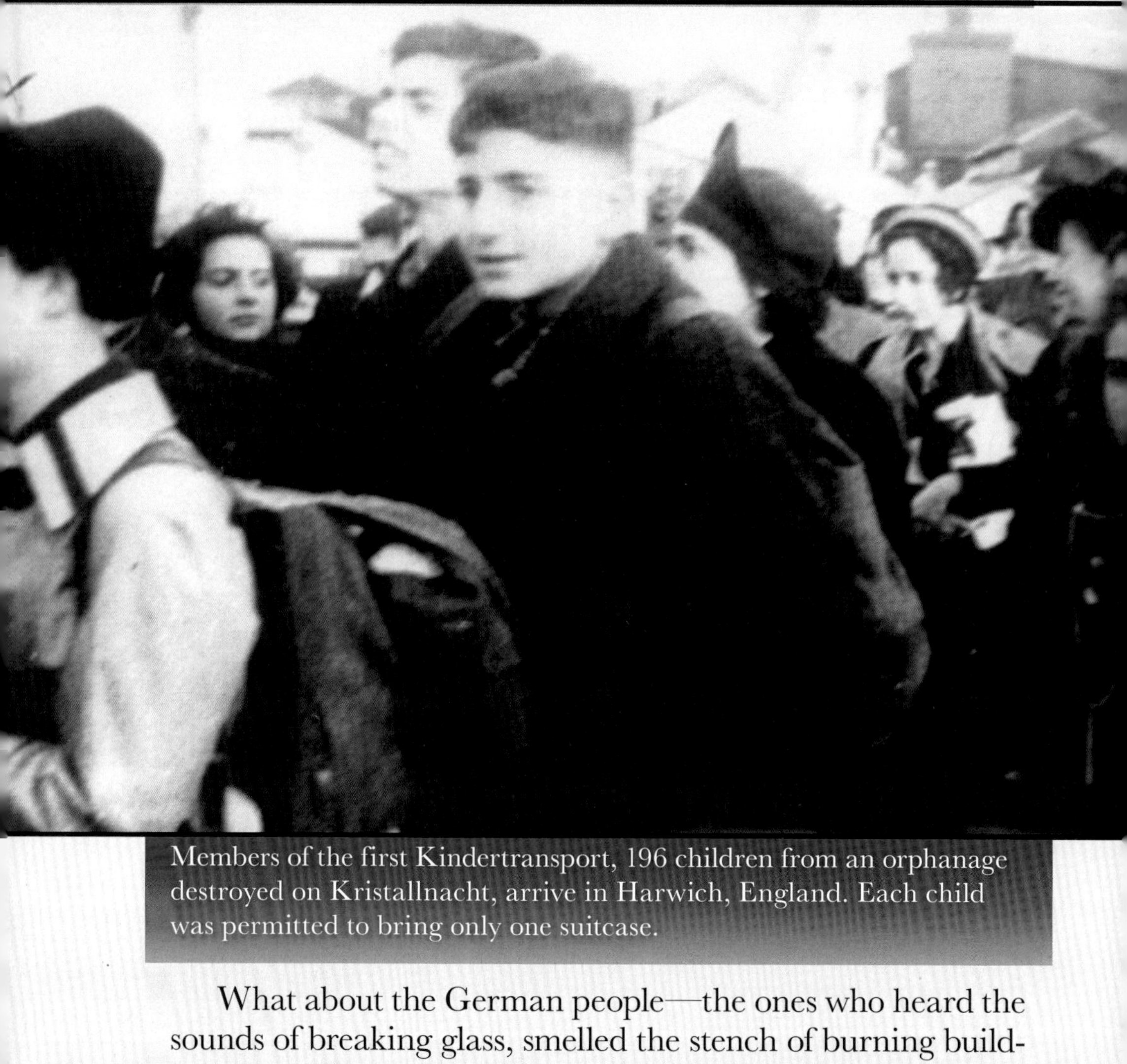

Members of the first Kindertransport, 196 children from an orphanage destroyed on Kristallnacht, arrive in Harwich, England. Each child was permitted to bring only one suitcase.

What about the German people—the ones who heard the sounds of breaking glass, smelled the stench of burning buildings, and witnessed the blows to the heads and backs of their neighbors? The American journalist William Shirer, author of *The Rise and Fall of the Third Reich: A History of Nazi Germany*, who was living in Berlin, saw the answer for himself:

> **Individually...many Germans were as horrified by the November 9 inferno as were Americans and Englishmen and other foreigners. But neither the leaders of the**

Christian churches nor the generals nor any other representatives of the "good" Germany spoke out at once in open protest.

ALL-OUT WAR

The failure of people to speak out made it possible for the Nazis to brutalize the Jews and drive many out of Germany. But Hitler had a far more sinister goal in mind, a goal the Nazis referred to as the "Final Solution" to what they regarded as the Jewish problem. In at least five separate speeches to large audiences, Hitler had promised "the annihilation of the Jewish race throughout Europe." His ultimate goal was to somehow exterminate all the Jews on the continent.

But as long as the world was watching, he could not carry out his plan. The cold-blooded murder of millions of people required secrecy. Hitler found that secrecy in the wastelands of eastern Poland under the concealing fog of war.

Ten months after Kristallnacht, the German army invaded Poland, launching the Second World War. Hitler's idea was for Germany to spread out into western Poland and for eastern Poland to be the dumping ground—and eventually the killing ground—for the Jews. The Nazis had a well-planned system for their diabolic scheme. In the areas they conquered, they herded the Jews into tiny, horribly crowded neighborhoods called "ghettos." They built walls around the ghettos and set up workshops, forcing the imprisoned Jews to produce clothing, armaments, supplies, and other items for their enemies. Periodically they "thinned" the ghettos, transporting large groups "to the east."

To the east were the concentration camps. At first the camps were slave labor centers, places where Jews were

Jewish women and children stand next to the railroad cattle cars that brought them to the extermination camp in Auschwitz, Poland. More than one million people were killed here.

concentrated in large numbers and made to perform whatever labor the Reich needed. Many died in the labor camps through backbreaking toil, starvation, exposure, punishment, and the cruelty of sadistic guards. Eventually four camps were built and two slave labor camps expanded specifically to serve as annihilation centers, places whose primary purpose was murdering Jews. All six were in eastern Poland, away from the prying eyes of any who might object.

As the war raged, Germany took over other countries and more Jews fell under Nazi rule. They could not be killed where war correspondents might report the deeds. So in France, Belgium, and the Netherlands, transit camps were set up to hold Jews until they could be shipped to the extermination camps in the east. Eventually all the ghettos were "liquidated," all the transit camps emptied, and the extermination camps operated at full speed.

QUENCHING THE FLAMES

The war that allowed Hitler to pursue the Final Solution was also its undoing.

Germany lost the war before the Nazis could kill all the Jews still in the camps. One by one, from July 24, 1944, to May 8, 1945, the Allied armies liberated the camps and freed their prisoners. The world finally saw what the Nazis tried to keep secret.

As the revelations tumbled out in news reports, photographs, and personal testimonies, the world was stunned and repulsed. Two-thirds of the Jews of Europe—six million men, women, and children—had been brutally murdered. Five million non-Jewish civilians had also been killed. The acts were so detestable the Allies struggled with what to call them

Helmeted military policemen guard the main defendants at the first Nuremberg Trial. Three were found not guilty, seven were given prison terms, and twelve were sentenced to death.

in bringing their perpetrators to justice. They settled on the term "crimes against humanity."

Of course, the thousands of people who had so viciously mistreated their fellow human beings could not all be punished. Some, like Hitler, committed suicide rather than face their accusers. Some died by other means, and some escaped. Hundreds of the worst who were caught were tried in dozens of trials beginning in Nuremberg in 1945. Some were executed and others imprisoned.

For the Jews who survived, recovery would be long and difficult. Many were left with physical scars that would plague them for the rest of their lives. Many would live with fear and emotional wounds that would never heal. All lost loved ones. But the survivors have been telling their stories, so the world will not forget. . . so people will understand that ideas and words lead to deeds, and twisted ideas and cruel words lead to ugly and harmful deeds. Nearly all the survivors from Germany who are speaking out begin their stories at the same place: Kristallnacht, the Night of Broken Glass.

Timeline

November 11, 1918 A newly installed civilian government of Germany agrees to an armistice, ending the fighting of World War I.

June 28, 1919 On the five-year anniversary of the incident that began World War I, the Treaty of Versailles is signed, imposing harsh penalties on Germany and requiring Germany to admit guilt in starting the war.

November 1923 After the failed Beer Hall Putsch, Hitler is imprisoned for treason, where he dictates his autobiography, *Mein Kampf.*

January 30, 1933 German President Paul von Hindenburg appoints Adolf Hitler chancellor of Germany.

February 27, 1933 The Reichstag is set on fire. The fire is blamed on Communists, although evidence suggests Nazis started the fire on orders from Hitler.

March 22, 1933 Dachau, the first concentration camp, located outside Munich, is opened and ready to receive detainees.

March 23, 1933 The Enabling Act is passed, giving Hitler, as chancellor, sweeping legislative powers.

April 1, 1933 A Nazi-led boycott of Jewish businesses begins overt government-sponsored persecution of Jews.

April 7, 1933–August 1, 1939 More than four hundred laws are passed imposing restrictions upon Jews and other groups.

September 15, 1935 Nazi leaders announce the Nuremberg Laws, a series of decrees that deprive Jews of citizenship and many rights.

March 13, 1938 Germany's annexation of Austria, a move called the *Anschluss*, begins the forced emigration of Jews from the Reich.

July 6-15, 1938 At Evian Conference, leaders from thirty-two countries refuse to admit Jewish refugees from Germany.

October 28, 1938 Deportation order is issued forcing Polish Jews to return to Poland.

November 7, 1938 Herschel Grynszpan assassinates Ernst vom Rath, a German diplomat, in Paris, France, giving the Nazis a pretext to begin the undisguised violent pogrom against Jews.

November 9–10, 1938 Nazis conduct a highly organized assault throughout Germany on Jewish businesses, synagogues, schools, and homes that come to be called *Kristallnacht*, the Night of Broken Glass.

November 12, 1938 The Decree on the Exclusion of Jews from German Economic Life makes Aryanization of Jewish businesses mandatory.

September 1, 1939 Germany invades Poland, beginning World War II.

January 20, 1942 At the Wannsee Conference, Nazi leaders articulate the Final Solution, already underway, since the opening of the first extermination camp in December 8, 1941.

May 8, 1945 The Allies accept Germany's unconditional surrender, ending World War II and putting a stop to the Holocaust.

November 20, 1945 An international tribunal begins the trials of war criminals at Nuremberg.

Glossary

ALLIES A group of nations fighting against Germany, Italy, and Japan in World War II, primarily Great Britain, the United States, France, and Russia.

ANTI-SEMITISM Prejudice against Jewish people.

BAYONET A steel blade attached to the barrel of a rifle.

BOLSHEVIK Communist.

BOYCOTT Refusal to buy the products or use the services of a group in order to protest the actions of that group.

COUP A sudden illegal takeover of a government.

EMIGRATION The act of leaving a country to live elsewhere.

FLEDGLING Just beginning, like a bird just learning to fly.

FÜHRER German word meaning leader.

GODSEND An unexpected event that works for one's benefit, as though God sent it for that purpose.

GOOSE STEP A military marching style in which the legs are raised high and the knees are not bent.

KEHILLA (plural: kehillot) A Jewish community, usually with structures that administer charity, cultural, and community affairs.

MARK German unit of currency.

ORATORY Art of public speaking.

POGROM An organized vicious attack on a particular group of people, usually officially sanctioned, characterized by massacres and destruction of property.

PROFESSION An occupation or career that requires formal education, prolonged training, and mastery of a body of knowledge, such as doctor, teacher, lawyer, or engineer.

SCAPEGOAT An innocent person or group that is blamed for something that is the fault of another.

STORM TROOPS Men of the *Sturmabteilung* (SA), the Nazi police force, also called "Brownshirts," eventually replaced by the *Schutzstaffel* (SS), also called "Blackshirts."

SUBVERT To undermine; to work against.

VORACIOUS Eager to consume a large amount of a particular item, such as food.

For More Information

International Raoul Wallenberg Foundation
34 East 67th Street
New York, NY 10065
(212) 737-3275
Website: http://www.raoulwallenberg.net
The International Raoul Wallenberg Foundation provides educational books, films, articles, and classroom resources promoting awareness of the people and groups who rescued Jews during the Holocaust.

Sarah and Chaim Neuberger Holocaust Education Centre
UJA Federation of Greater Toronto
Lipa Green Centre, Sherman Campus
4600 Bathurst Street, 4th Floor
Toronto, ON, M2R 3V2
Canada
(416) 631-5689
Website: http:// www. holocaustcentre.com
A part of the Jewish Museum of Canada, the Neuberger Holocaust Education Centre houses a museum, provides educational resources, preserves survivor testimonies, and sponsors programs that foster understanding and dialogue about the Holocaust.

Simon Wiesenthal Center
1399 South Roxbury Drive
Los Angeles, CA 90035
(310) 553-9036
Website: http://www.wiesenthal.com

The Simon Wiesenthal Center is a human rights agency that works against anti-Semitism, promotes human rights, and teaches about the Holocaust. It maintains three Museums of Tolerance, produces films, and offers access to a vast library of information about the Holocaust.

USC Shoah Foundation Institute for Visual History and Education
650 West 35th Street, Suite 114
Los Angeles, CA 90089-2571
(213) 740-6001
Website: http://sfi.usc.edu
The Shoah Foundation is a research and education institution that seeks "to overcome prejudice, intolerance, and bigotry" by capturing and preserving video testimonies of survivors of the Holocaust. The foundation also includes testimonies of survivors of genocides other than the Holocaust.

U.S. Holocaust Memorial Museum
100 Raoul Wallenberg Place SW
Washington, DC 20024-2126
(202) 488-0400
Website: http://www.ushmm.org
The U.S. Holocaust Memorial Museum is America's national institution for the documentation, study, and

interpretation of Holocaust history and serves as this country's memorial to the millions of people murdered during the Holocaust.

Yad Vashem
Holocaust Martyrs' and Heroes' Remembrance Authority
Har Hazikaron
P.O. Box 3477
Jerusalem 9103401
Israel
(972-2) 644-3574
Website: http://www.yadvashem.org
Yad Vashem is the "world center for documentation, research, education, and commemoration of the Holocaust." It is a collection of museums and a repository for documents, exhibitions, photographs, and comprehensive information about the Holocaust.

WEBSITES

Due to the changing nature of Internet links, Rosen Publishing has developed an online list of websites related to the subject of this book. This site is updated regularly. Please use this link to access the list:

http://www.rosenlinks.com/DHH/Krist

For Further Reading

Altman, Linda Jacobs. *Hidden Teens, Hidden Lives: Primary Sources from the Holocaust*. Berkeley Heights, NJ: Enslow Publishers, 2010.

Altman, Linda Jacobs. *Shattered Youth in Nazi Germany: Primary Sources from the Holocaust*. Berkeley Heights, NJ: Enslow Publishers, 2010.

Bard, Mitchell G. *48 Hours of Kristallnacht: Night of Destruction/Dawn of the Holocaust: An Oral History*. Guilford, CT: Lyons Press, 2008.

Byers, Ann. *Courageous Teen Resisters: Primary Sources from the Holocaust*. Berkeley Heights, NJ: Enslow Publishers, 2010.

Byers, Ann. *Rescuing the Danish Jews: A Heroic Story from the Holocaust*. Berkeley Heights, NJ: Enslow Publishers, 2012.

Byers, Ann. *Saving Children from the Holocaust: The Kindertransport*. Berkeley Heights, NJ: Enslow Publishers, 2012.

Byers, Ann. *Trapped—Youth in the Nazi Ghettos: Primary Sources from the Holocaust*. Berkeley Heights, NJ: Enslow Publishers, 2010.

Byers, Ann. *Youth Destroyed—The Nazi Camps: Primary Sources from the Holocaust*. Berkeley Heights, NJ: Enslow Publishers, 2010.

Cooper, Mark A. *Edelweiss Pirates: Operation Einstein*. West Conshohocken, PA: Infinity, 2012.

Darman, Peter. *The Holocaust and Life Under Nazi Occupation*. New York, NY: Rosen Publishing, 2012.

Deem, James. *Kristallnacht: The Nazi Terror That Began the Holocaust*. Berkeley Heights, NJ: Enslow Publishers, 2011.

Freeman, Charles. *Why Did the Rise of the Nazis Happen?* Milwaukee, WI: Gareth Stevens, 2010.

Gerhardt, Uta, and Thomas Karlauf, eds. *The Night of Broken Glass: Eyewitness Accounts of Kristallnacht*. Malden, MA: Polity Press, 2012.

Kirsch, Jonathan. *The Short, Strange Life of Herschel Grynszpan: A Boy Avenger, a Nazi Diplomat, and a Murder in Paris*. New York, NY: Liveright, 2013.

Mara, Wil. *Kristallnacht: Nazi Persecution of the Jews in Europe*. Dundee, OR: Benchmark, 2009.

Meyer, Beate, Hermann Simon, and Chana Schütz, eds. *Jews in Nazi Berlin: From Kristallnacht to Liberation*. Chicago, IL: University of Chicago Press, 2009.

Sharenow, Robert. *The Berlin Boxing Club*. Reprint ed. New York, NY: HarperCollins, 2011.

Sheehan, Sean. *Why Did the Holocaust Happen?* Milwaukee, WI: Gareth Stevens, 2010.

Stille, Darlene. *Architects of the Holocaust*. Oakland, CA: CompassPoint, 2011.

Voorhoeve, Anne C. *My Family for the War*. New York, NY: Dial Books, 2012.

Bibliography

Bankier, David, and Israel Gutman, eds. *Nazi Europe and the Final Solution*. Jerusalem, Israel: Yad Vashem, 2003.

Distal, Barbara, and Ruth Jakusch, eds. *Concentration Camp Dachau 1933–1945*. Brussels, Belgium: Comité International de Dachau, 1978.

Drescher, Ruth. Transcript of address to Seton Hill University's Annual Kristallnacht Remembrance Interfaith Service, National Catholic Center for Holocaust Education, November 8, 2005. Retrieved January 17, 2008 (http://blogs.setonhill.edu/ncche/014329.php).

Gilbert, Martin. *Kristallnacht: Prelude to Destruction*. New York, NY: HarperCollins, 2006.

Grynszpan, Zindel. Testimony at trial of Adolf Eichmann, Session 014-04. District Court of Jerusalem, April 11-August 14, 1961. Retrieved August 20, 2013 (http://www.nizkor.org/ftp.cgi/people/e/eichmann.adolf/transcripts/ftp.cgi?people/e/eichmann.adolf/transcripts/Sessions/Session-014-04).

Harris, Mark Jonathan, and Deborah Oppenheimer. *Into the Arms of Strangers: Stories of the Kindertransport*. New York, NY: MFJ Books, 2000.

Herz, Yitzhak Sophoni "Kristallnacht at the Dinslaken Orphanage." *Yad Vashem Studies*, XI, 1976, pp. 345–349.

Hiemer, Ernst. *Der Giftpilz* (*The Poisonous Mushroom*). Retrieved August 8, 2013 (http://vho.org/aaargh/fran/livres10/PoisonMush.pdf).

Holocaust Education and Archive Research Team. *Zbaszyn: Deportation to the Border Town Camp –1938*. Retrieved August 6, 2013 (http://www.holocaustresearchproject.org/holoprelude/Zbaszyn.html).

Jewish Virtual Library. "Kristallnacht Order, November 10, 1938." Retrieved August 6, 2013 (http://www.jewishvirtuallibrary.org/jsource/Holocaust/kristallnacht_order.html).

Praeger, Peter. Testimony before USC Shoah Foundation, May 24, 2012. Retrieved August 15, 2013 (http://www.youtube.com/watch?v=RGNGwXzs9tQ).

Shirer, William L. *The Rise and Fall of the Third Reich: A History of Nazi Germany*. New York, NY: Simon & Schuster, 1959.

Steinhardt, Carola. Oral History Interview, U.S. Holocaust Memorial Museum, RG-50.030*0368, June 3, 1996. Retrieved August 15, 2013 (http://collections.ushmm.org/artifact/image/h00/00/h0000261.pdf).

Swarsensky, Manfred. "A Rabbi Recalls Kristallnacht in Berlin." Transcript of audio interview with Wisconsin Historical Society. Retrieved August 22, 2013 (http://www.wisconsinhistory.org/HolocaustSurvivors/excerpts/003779.asp).

U.S. Holocaust Memorial Museum. "Antisemitic Legislation, 1933–1939." *Holocaust Encyclopedia*. Retrieved August 8, 2013 (http://www.ushmm.org/wlc/en/article.php?ModuleId=10007901).

U.S. Holocaust Memorial Museum. "German Jewish Refugees, 1933–1939." *Holocaust Encyclopedia*. Retrieved

August 8, 2013 (http://www.ushmm.org/wlc/en/article.php?ModuleId=10005468).

U.S. Holocaust Memorial Museum. "Voyage of the St. Louis." *Holocaust Encyclopedia*. Retrieved August 20, 2013 (http://www.ushmm.org/wlc/en/article.php?ModuleId=10005267).

White Rose Society. "The Second Leaflet." Retrieved January 14, 2009 (http://www.whiterosesociety.org/WRS_pamphets_second.html).

Index

ABOUT THE AUTHOR

Ann Byers is a teacher, youth worker, writer, and editor with a passion for history. This is her ninth book on the Holocaust. Byers lives in California.

PHOTO CREDITS

Cover (clockwise from top left) Galerie Bilderwelt/Hulton Archive /Getty Images, Hulton Archive/Getty Images, © iStockphoto.com /Steve Christensen, Fred Ramage/Hulton Archive/Getty Images; pp. 4–5 United States Holocaust Memorial Museum, courtesy of Lynne Ravas; p. 8 LTL/Universal Images Group/Getty Images; p. 10 Buyenlarge/Archive Photos/Getty Images; p. 12 Keystone /Hulton Archive/Getty Images; pp. 14, 19 Hulton Archive/Archive Photos/Getty Images; pp. 17, 32–33 Imagno/Hulton Archive /Getty Images, pp. 22, 28 Mondadori/Getty Images; pp. 23, 54–55 FPG/Archive Photos/Getty Images; p. 30 Anthony Potter Collection /Archive Photos/Getty Images; pp. 34–35, 40, 60–61 Universal Images Group/Getty Images; pp. 37, 45, 47 © AP Images; pp. 38–39 Keystone-France/Gamma-Keystone/Getty Images; p. 43 AFP /Getty Images; pp. 52–53 United States Holocaust Memorial Museum, courtesy of Robert A. Schmuhl; p. 58 United States Holocaust Memorial Museum, courtesy of Frances Rose; p. 62 Agentur Voller Ernst/picture-alliance/dpa/AP Images; cover and interior page background elements optimarc/Shutterstock.com (gray textures), Gallup Pix/Photodisc/Thinkstock (pillars), Gubin Yury/Shutterstock.com (barbed wire).

Designer: Brian Garvey; Editor: Kathy Kuhtz Campbell;
Photo Researcher: Cindy Reiman